Walking Into Your Destiny By Faith

Nikeya Quick

REJOICE
Essential Publishing

Nikeya Quick/Rejoice Essential Publishing
PO BOX 512

Effingham, SC 29541
www.republishing.org

Unless otherwise indicated, scripture is taken from the King James Version.'

All Scripture marked with the designation "GW" is taken from GOD'S WORD®.© 1995, 2003, 2013, 2014, 2019, 2020 by God's Word to the Nations Mission Society. Used by permission.

The Holy Bible, Berean Study Bible, BSB Copyright ©2016, 2020 by Bible Hub Used by Permission. All Rights Reserved Worldwide.

Scripture taken from the New King James Version®. Copyright © 1982 by Thomas Nelson. Used by permission. All rights reserved.

Walking Into Your Destiny By Faith/Nikeya Quick

ISBN-13: 978-1-956775-25-9

TABLE OF CONTENTS

Introduction

*H*EBREWS 11:1-2 (KJB), "Now faith is the substance of things hoped for, the evidence of things not seen. For by it the elders obtained a good report."

Faith's definition in the Strong's Concordance is the Greek word Pistis, it is a feminine noun and means conviction of the truth of anything, belief; in the NT of conviction or belief respecting man's relationship to God and divine things, generally with the included idea of trust and holy fervour born of faith and joined with it, this is in relation with God and Christ (Blue Letter Bible, 2021).

We have been taught this Scripture in Sunday service, Bible studies, devotion times, seminars, and so on. Just reading the Scripture alone is self-explanatory. But when it is time to apply the Scripture, it can be a struggle. Faith is not in what we think logically or even in what we know. It is simply having confidence or assurance that something is going to happen. The example that we have is when Jesus told the disciples in Matthew 17:20 (GWT), "He told them, because you have faith so little faith. I can guarantee this truth: If your faith is the size of a mustard seed, you can say to this mountain, move from here to there, and it will move. Nothing will be impossible for you." A mustard seed is one of the smallest seeds and it can grow to be one of the biggest trees in the world. So, Jesus is telling us that we don't need a lot of faith. We just need enough to show Him that we believe His word. I always wondered why the Lord only required us to have mustard seed faith. So, I asked one day. The response I received is that He knows faith is a supernatural substance and we live in a natural world, in a natural body, and we depend on natural things. We also deal with natural and tangible problems that we see and experience with our natural minds. We believe in God within our spirit and not in natural logic. With that being said, when we have so many natural things working for us or against us, it can be a challenge to believe what we cannot see. The Lord only requires a small substance of faith, assurance, and confidence in Him.

I'm immediately taken to Matthew 18:3 (BSB), which says, "Truly I tell you, unless you change and become like little children, you will never enter the kingdom of heaven." When looking at this Scripture, the Bible illustrates that a child believes in his or her parents by what they are taught and they depend on their parents for everything or else they will perish. That is confidence and assurance. For example, children depend on their parents to eat, keep them clean, go to school, and to go to sleep. The list goes on and on. The Lord wants us to depend on Him for everything. We have to know that if the Lord doesn't do it for us, it won't happen for us, just like the little children. We must trust Him at His word. As we show Him that we believe in Him, and follow His instructions, then He does the rest.

I remember years ago, I was in the process of divorce and it was finalized. I had been separated from my ex-husband for a year or so and wanted to rebuild my life. I realized that no matter how hard I tried to make things come together on my own, they weren't. I remember being so frustrated with my life. I began to rationalize with why people would rather die than live. I had not contemplated suicide, but I thought in some cases to die could be better than to live. This was a deception from the enemy and a seed of suicide that was planted in a time of hopelessness. I became frustrated and started to look for validation elsewhere. I had started to date this guy casually. He was very kind, giving, and thoughtful. This was the opposite of my ex-husband. After about four weeks of dating the guy, I knew that he wasn't the one for me. Something was missing from this very kind, thoughtful, and giving guy. I felt it in my inner being. I had wasted enough time in my previous marriage of 5 years and being together for 13 years. I was determined not to waste that amount of time again. Besides, I was almost in my mid-thirties at this point. I allowed the guy to take me out on the last date. After dinner, we pulled up to my house and he walked me to my car, which was parked in the driveway. He was about to kiss me and I would not allow him to. As he leaned in to kiss me, this strong feeling wailed up from my belly and was screaming NO! This isn't it! I kindly backed away from the young man and the words came flying out of my mouth. "I'm sorry, but you are not it!" I looked at my house and pointed at it saying, "This isn't it," and then I pointed to my car and said, "This isn't it either." The words came flying out of my mouth with boldness, confidence, and assurance so much that the guy apologized to me and he left. I had never experienced that before. The feeling I had in my belly and the assurance I spoke with were of Faith in God. My inner man spoke up for me and I believed. The frustration I felt during this time of hopelessness was pushing me closer to the Lord and my destiny.

After that day, I began to attend church regularly and submitted my life to the Lord. I was currently in a backslidden state. Shortly after submitting my life to the Lord, I received the Baptism of the Holy Spirit. The Holy Spirit began to give me instructions. I remember sitting at my computer in my home and hearing the word "Move." I thought I was hearing things. But a few moments later, I heard again, "You're moving!" I knew then I was hearing the Lord speak to me and that He was giving me instructions. I jumped up with excitement and told my three boys. I didn't know at that point whether we were moving down the street, in the same city, state, or country. I had confidence and assurance in the Lord. I began to search for houses locally with several resources and even viewed a few homes. None of the homes I viewed was within my financial means at the time. I continued to look and serve the Lord and carry on with my daily routine.

I began to follow a well-known Prophet at the time and he was having a prophetic conference in Charlotte, North Carolina on a Friday night. I felt it in my spirit that I needed to be there. I attended the conference. During the conference, the prophet was speaking about a place called "There." He said, "The place called 'There' is the place where the Lord has all of the promises He made to you such as Husband/Wife, Dream Career, Business, etc." I left the conference with the assurance that this was confirmation of what the Lord had spoken to me about moving. I began to have an unction that Charlotte, North Carolina was the city the Lord wanted me to move to. I began to visit and apply for jobs. On my way to an interview, as I was driving down Interstate 85 South, I felt a love for the city as if I knew it. The Lord began to give me a vision of the promises He had given me years ago: the husband I dreamed of, a little girl that I always prayed for, me working in ministry with other women, and empowering other women. I moved to Charlotte, North Carolina and these things are coming to pass because I believed the Lord. I have received healing and deliverance in many areas of my life because of my obedience.

CHAPTER 1

Mustard Seed Faith

MATTHEW 17:20 (KJB) "AND Jesus said unto them, Because of your unbelief: for verily I say unto you, if ye have faith as a grain of a mustard seed, ye shall say unto this mountain, Remove hence to yonder place; and it shall remove; and nothing shall be impossible unto you."

Having faith as small as a mustard seed sounds easy. A mustard seed is one of the smallest seeds on the earth. It is a round seed about 1 to 2 millimeters in diameter and is either a yellowish-white or black color. You can literally hold it on the tip of your finger. It sounds like it is easy to get that type of faith but it actually requires some testing to get this type of faith. It may not take a hard test or trial but simply following the instructions of the Lord and believing that He will do what He says. Jesus spoke the parable of the mustard seed faith because a man brought his son to His disciples to be healed and delivered from a tormenting demon, but they could not. Jesus was disappointed in His disciples, and He healed the boy. Jesus's response to His disciples was that they were a "faithless and perverse generation." Faithless means without belief or unbelief. You will not achieve anything if you do not have faith, assurance, or confidence that it is possible. The reason for salvation is to be saved by Jesus, to have God as your Father and the Holy Spirit as your helper, and to receive eternal life. If you have received salvation, and you do not believe that asking God, "Abba" our Father, that He will hear your prayers and will answer them in His Son, "Jesus Christ our Savior." It is in Jesus Christ's name that He will do it for you. Is your salvation in vain? Why would you need a God, a Savior, or a Helper? Jesus said in John 14:13-14 (KJB), "And whatsoever ye shall ask in my name, that will I do, that the Father may be glorified in the Son, v14 If ye shall ask anything in my name, I will do it." How amazing is that? For Jesus to allow us to use His name in our prayers and that He will do what we ask in His name so that our Father will be glorified. Hallelujah! That gives you confidence, assurance, and faith in the name of Jesus.

Believing God for a new job, a new home, passing a test, renewal of a relationship, being healed, deliverance, a renewed mind, children being set free are all great things. Trusting in Him gives us the advantage over our natural lives or living without Him. In order to believe in God, you have to take a chance and speak in faith. Even if you are not sure of the results of the instructions of the Lord with your natural mind, you must believe in your spirit that you can trust God. You can believe Him at His Word. In Isaiah 55:10-11, God is telling us that the rain that falls from the sky and the snow does not return back to the sky but it accomplishes the will of God, such as causing seeds in the ground to bud and to provide bread for us, it is the same way with His Word. So we must believe the Lord knows more than we do and He can see farther and higher than what we can see. One of the names of God is "El-Roi." He is the God of Seeing. He is our Creator! He formed and fashioned you. He knows your efficiencies and inefficiencies. So faith takes trusting in Him.

Some of us are so used to making everything happen on our own. We operate like this in our household, on our jobs, businesses, and in our families. We are quick to take the initiative because no one else will. We solve problems for everyone and everything. Then we get saved and try to operate the same way, but we don't trust God. No faith in God makes your salvation perverse. Going back to Matthew 17:17, Jesus called the disciples a "faithless and perverse generation." Perverse in the Strong's Concordance is the Greek word "Diastrepho." It means to distort, turn aside, oppose, and plot against God's saving purposes and plans. To turn aside from the right path, to pervert or corrupt. The perversion that Jesus is speaking about is the disciples not using the power that He gave them to use His name correctly. I believe the disciples were without Jesus at the time the boy's father approached them and they saw the boy being vexed by the demon and they allowed it to make them afraid so they did not think they had the power to minister deliverance and healing to the boy. The boy's father was smart enough to go to the source of healing and deliverance! The person whose name was supposed to cause his son to be healed and whole. This displeased Jesus that the very ones whom He has chosen to do the works of the Lord with Him, didn't believe or didn't trust, didn't have confidence, and assurance in His name over something that looked worse than anything they had ever seen before. He knew that He came to fulfill the will of the Father but to leave His power in us here on earth. It only takes mustard seed faith to do what the Lord has called us to do. We can start working on this by following the first command of God, trusting that if we follow Him, He can't fail, that it has to happen because He told us that His Word will not return to Him without fulfilling what He said it would. God does not ask us to do anything that we are not capable of doing, what is not already done, and what is not already inside of us.

CHAPTER 2

Faith's Foundation

ROMANS 8:15 (KJB) "FOR ye have not received the spirit of bondage again to fear; but ye have received the Spirit of adoption, whereby we cry, "Abba, Father."

The foundation to having faith in God is knowing Him and having a relationship with Him. "Abba" means father and our love. Knowing that He is a good Father, He called you "Beloved" which means He loved you first. There is nothing you did to deserve or earn His love for you. He has your best interest at heart. He is the same God today, yesterday, and forevermore. We must know that He is not a God that will or could lie. God does not change His mind about you, and He would never lead you astray or into danger. The "Love" of the Father "Abba" should be your very source that fuels your obedience in hearing His voice and obeying His commands.

Some people have experienced betrayal and abandonment from their natural mother or father, so they only listen to some of what their parents tell them. Then they accept Jesus Christ as their Lord and Savior and treat Abba like they do their own natural mother or father. How do I know this? Because I am one who once treated the Lord this way. When the Lord began to reveal to me how good of a Father He is, it broke my heart because I did not know that I was saying," Lord, I trust some of what you are saying, but I'm not going to follow every command because I need to make sure I'm protecting myself from being deceived by You, or tricked into doing something that will eventually harm me." Instantly, He was my God, Father, and Lord. I no longer doubted His love for me. To treat someone who gave His only "Begotten Son," the only Son He had, for my sins and to shed His blood, He accepted me into His kingdom and called me "Beloved" with no other requirements besides accepting His Son as my Savior. God offered me so many wonderful benefits that will last for eternity. This is quite an eye-opening experience. But I could not allow the devil to cause me to feel condemned. I simply repented to the Lord for treating Him in such a manner and asked for His forgiveness, and I received my "Sonship." I learned that the Lord only instructs us to do things for our best interest, even if it hurts our flesh. Our goal is eternal life, our flesh dies daily, but our inner man is renewed day by day.

An example of the love of the Father for us is illustrated in John 15:8-9 (NKJV), "By this My Father is glorified, that you bear much fruit; so you will be My disciples. v9 As the Father loved Me, I also have loved you; abide in My love." The love of the Father is shown to us through His Son, Jesus Christ. Love in Strong's Concordance is the Greek word "agape," which means affection, goodwill, love, benevolence, brotherly love, and love feasts.

The love that Jesus is speaking of here is only conditioned on the fact of you abiding in Him, receiving Him as your Lord and Savior, continuing to keep His commands, and loving others as He has loved you. The requirement is to receive His love and give His love. This is the true meaning of love. Our Faith is fueled by love. We receive His love and are required to give it as well.

Let's talk about "Son-ship." Abba is our Father and now we are "sons" of God. We must accept our adoption by faith according to Romans 8:15-23. When we become sons of God, we are also heirs of God. Everything God offered to His Son Jesus, He has offered to us. We will never be the Savior or sit at His right hand, but we will obtain eternal life in Heaven and receive the benefits of God. Romans 8:14 specifies that only those who are led by the Spirit of God are the Sons of God. In order to be a true Son of God you listen and follow Him. In the Book of 1 Kings chapter 17, are numerous examples of Elijah the Prophet trusting in God for so many things. Elijah had such great faith to speak to the King of Israel, Ahab, and pronounce that there will be no dew or rain for these years, but according to his word. At Elijah's word, there was no rain. Even as Elijah spoke this, he was a first partaker of this drought. But the Lord sustained Elijah. He gave Elijah instructions on where to hide so that he could provide water for him and food. Elijah followed the instructions of God and he was fed by ravens and was able to drink fresh water from a brook. After the brook dried up, the Lord instructed Elijah to go to Zarephath in Sidon and dwell there because he had instructed a widow woman to sustain him. This is a true example of being led by the Spirit of God. It is a wonderful thing to be a Son of God.

CHAPTER 3

The Desire to Believe God

Mark 9:24 (KJB) "And straightway the father of the child cried out, and said with tears, Lord, I believe; help thou mine unbelief."

"Believe" in this Scripture is the Greek word "Pisteuo" which means to think to be true, to be persuaded of, to credit, place confidence in. "Unbelief" in this Scripture is the Greek word "Apistia" and means unfaithfulness, faithless, want of faith, unbelief, and weakness of faith. We must have a desire to believe in God in order for our faith to manifest and to produce fruit. The Word of God says in Psalms 20:4 (KJB), "Grant thee according to thine own heart, and fulfil all thy counsel." So, the Lord rewards us according to the desires in our hearts. In the same story of the father who brought his son to Jesus because the disciples could not cast the demon out of him, the father had enough faith to bring him to Jesus because he heard that Jesus could heal him. In Mark 9:23-24, Jesus asked the boy's father if he believed that he could cast it out and replied to the father that if thou canst believe, all things are possible to him that believeth. The man cries out to Jesus with tears, "Lord, I believe; help my unbelief." Although you don't believe all the time, our Father is compassionate enough to help you in your weak areas of faith.

In Ephesians 14:1, we are encouraged to follow after charity and desire spiritual gifts, but rather that ye may prophesy. The gift of faith is listed as one of the gifts of the Spirit in 1 Corinthians 12:9. Although this is a gift, it also is a requirement of the Lord in order for us to please Him. It is impossible for our salvation to please the Father if we are not trusting and believing that He can do what He says He will do for us or that we even trust in His plans for our lives.

The Lord loves for us to trust that He is who He says He is.

We are constantly reminded of how He can provide for us all throughout the Bible: from the Old Testament to the end of the New Testament. You will find in the Old Testament many instances where the Israelites had to trust in God for food, water, land to live on, and victory in battle. In the Book of Joshua chapter 1, before Joshua led the children of Israel to the battle of Jericho, the Lord gave him instructions to be strong and of good courage in order for him to give them the land of their inheritance that He promised them in the wilderness as Moses was leading them. The Lord gave commands for them to keep His Word in their mouths so they will prosper wherever they go. If the children of Israel did not believe and listen to the instructions the Father gave them, the walls of Jericho would not have fallen down and they would not have taken the victory. They had the belief that Hebrews 11:6 (KJB) references: "But without faith it is impossible to please him: for he that cometh to God must believe that he is, and that he is a rewarder of them that diligently seek him."

I believe as we desire to trust God's plans for our lives that He makes it easy for us to trust in Him. He does this through His track record with us. From times as small as needing gas in your car, to having to stand on Philippians 4:19 (KJB) which says, "But my God shall supply all of your need according to his riches in glory by Christ Jesus." We believed this by faith and guess what? You checked your checking account and there is money there that was unexpected. Even the time when you picked out a home that was well above what you thought you could afford, but the lender contacted you and you are approved and the mortgage payment is affordable for you. The Lord is a Good God. He loves us and only wants the very best for us. Even as we desire to trust God and follow His commands, this causes our faith to grow. That mustard seed faith will grow into the mustard tree eventually.

There are many women and men of God that are called "men and women of Faith." They received this title not because they are Pastors,

Apostles, Teachers, Preachers, or Leaders. It is because they believed and trusted in God. Living a life of faith and not operating by the system of the world, they knew that with God, all things are possible. Jesus lets us know in Mark 10:27 (KJB), "With men it is impossible, but not with God: for with God all things are possible." We must know that God can do anything.

CHAPTER 4

Faith's Muscle

GALATIANS 5:6 (KJB) "FOR in Jesus Christ neither circumcision avai-
leth anything, nor uncircumcision;
but faith which worketh by love."

The strength of our faith is love. If we don't
operate out of love, our faith will not work. You
can believe in God for a new car, but if you are
not operating in love towards the people around
you, whether they are nice to you or not, you
won't get your new car until your heart is right
towards that person. Proverbs 4:23 (KJB) says,
"Keep thy heart with all diligence; for out of it
are the issues of life."

I learned a few years back to guard my heart
pertaining to how I responded to people who

upset, frustrated, or mistreated me. I asked the Lord to help me with this because I didn't find it fair to forgive someone who hurts or mistreats us. I thought to myself, "Where is the justice?" I wanted to be recompensed for the hurt and pain. But that's not how justice works in the Kingdom of God. Justice is given by God at what He thinks is the best action and response on how to handle the issue and when He is going to avenge you. Romans 12:19 (KJB) says, "Dearly beloved, avenge not yourselves, but rather give place unto wrath: for it is written, Vengeance is mine; I will repay saith the Lord." The Father is telling us to allow others to mistreat, hurt, or persecute us, but be good to them because the Lord will avenge us. Romans 12:14 (KJB) says, "Bless them which persecute you, bless, and curse not." In order to keep my love walk strong so that my faith will work, I always remember to have my heart in the right place. I will expound on guarding your heart. Now that we have a foundation for justice on wrong doing, we can guard our hearts knowing that the Lord sees and knows everything concerning us. He cares about what bothers and hurts us. In order to guard your heart, you must not focus on how the person you are interacting with is responding to you. Not allowing them to cause you to react or respond outside of the will of God, watching what you say and do, and protecting the things you care deeply about.

We must always operate out of a pure heart, having a good conscience. In Acts 24:16, the Apostle Paul tells us that he exercise's himself to always have a conscience void of offense toward God, and toward men in hope of the resurrection. Not allowing someone to offend you is a great way to guard your heart. It may hurt your feelings or make you angry at what someone else says or does. You should always address that situation in love. In most cases, I will apologize for upsetting that person or try to make the situation as peaceful as possible, still operating in truth and love. We have to show mercy to others. Everyone is not in the place you are in your walk with Christ and some are not even saved that we deal with on an everyday basis. You cannot expect them to respond to you in a Godly manner or sometimes even out of love, if you do get offended. Get offense out of your heart quickly. I usually go ahead and address the spirit of offense directly. I will say, "I rebuke you spirit of offense! You cannot operate in my life! I am not easily offended in the name of Jesus!" Once I'm finished, I go ahead and forgive that person for what they said or did to offend me or make me upset, so that I get that out of my heart right away. You do not want bitterness to set in because bitterness creates a wall or barrier that will require deliverance. After I forgive them, I speak that I love them, and pray blessings over the person. Now it is completely out of my heart and when I look at the person, I don't look at them as a bad person. Honestly, when you genuinely pray for someone and speak blessings over them, the Lord will make your heart sensitive to why the person responds that way and you will have compassion on that person and maybe add them to your daily prayer list and hope to see the salvation of the Lord or see the Lord glorified in their life.

Now I have protected my heart from hatred, anger, bitterness, and offense. All of these things can hinder your faith from operating. If the enemy tries to bring it back to your mind to cause you to have emotions or feelings about the situation again, you rebuke him all over again. James

4:7 (KJB) says, "Submit yourselves therefore to God. Resist the devil and he will flee from you." Once he sees that he cannot make you angry or upset at the person and have hatred, unforgiveness, and bitterness in your heart, he will leave you alone about it. Now your conscience is void of the offense. Romans 12:9 (KJB) says, "Let love be without dissimulation. Abhor that which is evil; cleave to that which is good." Dissimulation means concealment of one's thoughts, feelings, or character. Basically that is deceit or dishonesty. That is why you should not pretend that what the person said or did does not bother or hurt you. You need to address the issue in love. If you still have the issue, you go and purge yourself by repenting for allowing it in your heart and rebuke the spirit of offense all over again and pray for that person.

The love that the Lord requires us to operate in is fully described in 1 Corinthians 13:4-8. It states that "Charity" which is love, suffers long, and is kind; charity vaunts not itself, is not puffed up, it does not behave itself unseemly, seeks not her own, is not easily provoked, thinks no evil; does not rejoice in iniquity, but rejoices in the truth; it bears all things, hopes all things, endures all things. Charity never fails but whether there be prophecies they shall fail; whether there be tongues, they shall cease; whether there be knowledge, it shall vanish away. The Lord is telling us how he judges our love towards others and the love we have in our hearts ultimately. As I meditate on these Scriptures, it is like a mirror and I can tell you that it can make you say, "Ouch!" It shows you if you are really operating out of the love of God or Jesus Christ. I usually pray these Scriptures over myself and ask the Lord to give me the love He speaks of in these verses and I will go down the line of what the Scripture lists. So now that we know that we need love for faith to work, we must operate that way continuously.

Living By Faith

HEBREWS 10:38 (KJB), "NOW
the just shall live by faith: but if
any man draw back, my soul shall
have no pleasure in him."

We as believers should live by faith. The
word "live" means to spend one's life in a particular way or under particular circumstance or
to supply oneself with the means of subsistence,
according to Oxford's Live Dictionary. Living
by faith is simply relying on God and trusting
in Him for everything that we need. In Hebrews
chapter 11, it gives the history of the servants of
God and how they lived and obtained what was
promised to them by faith. I will say from my
own experience that living by faith is exciting
and can be very rewarding.

Faith is supernatural. When I rely on the Lord for something that I was not ordinarily supposed to obtain, my spirit leaps on the inside of me because I know that only God did it. I know that without Him, it could not have happened and that He is a good Father who loves and cares for me. Sharing the praise report with others, whether they are saved or not, increases my faith for something greater. I remember praying for the Lord to bless me with money to pay my cell phone bill. I prayed this prayer on Saturday night. I always stand on Philippians 4:19 when I ask the Lord for something. Philippians 4:19 (KJB) says, "And my God will supply all of your need, according to his riches in glory by Christ Jesus." Jesus has everything I need. I went to church the following Sunday morning. I walked in and spoke to all of my sisters and brothers at church and as I hugged one of my sisters in Christ, she said, "My husband and I have something for you." I said, "Okay." I forgot about the prayer the night before. I thought maybe they had a shirt for me, or a card or something. She walked over to me and gave me one hundred dollars! She said, "I don't know what you needed it for, but we are going to be obedient to the Lord." I told her it was for my phone bill. She smiled. I rejoiced in the Lord because He heard me when I asked Him and He did it! He provided for my needs according to His riches and glory. That boosted my faith level to continue to live by faith.

CHAPTER 6

Needs vs Lustful desires

JAMES 4:2-3 (KJB) "Ye lust, and have not: ye kill, and desire to have, and cannot obtain: ye fight and war, yet ye have not, because ye ask not. Ye ask and receive not, because ye ask amiss, that ye may consume it upon your lusts."

What is the difference between needs and lustful desires? Lustful desires or pleasures are not things you need to fulfill the plan of God for your life. Lustful desires only appeal to our flesh. An example of a lustful desire is wanting a Mercedes Benz so that you can seem important or appear to be doing well. That is a desire that would be considered vanity. It is vain.

It is to glorify yourself and not God. Don't get me wrong, there is nothing wrong with having a Mercedes Benz. It becomes wrong when you desire it to make it into an idol, for it to make your image look great, and to portray yourself as someone you are not. This is lustful. A need is when you need a car to get around in because you do not have one, or the car you have will not make it much longer. The Lord already knows your motives and intentions when you ask Him for something. He knows if it is a pure desire that will be used for His glory or if it is to glorify yourself. He will always bless you with what you ask for, when it is His desire and He knows that you are ready for it.

Sometimes, we don't receive the things we ask for because we are not ready for what we are asking for. Even the father of the prodigal son didn't want to give him his inheritance too soon because he knew that he was not mature enough to handle it, so it is with our "Abba" Father. He does not want to give you something that will in the end cause you harm or that you are not ready for.

I have learned to say, "Thank You" to God for the "No's" that I get for things that I have asked for even if it seems like I need it right now. There is a reason I am not getting it. Maturity may not always be the reason for you not getting it as well. The Lord may have something else in mind for you. A great example can be that you want a house that is a 3 bedroom 2 and a half bathroom in Fulton County, but He has a house for you that is a 5 bedroom 3 and a half bathroom located in Charleston County. At the appointed time, you would find the house, connect to the realtor and everything will be a smooth flow from there.

I have learned not to be forceful when it comes to trying to obtain something. An example is, you apply for a loan at 2 places and they say that you are not approved. You apply at a third place and they deny you for the same reason, such as your credit score. Now you are racking up points taken from your credit score for applying. Instead of applying over and over again and getting denied, seek the Lord and ask Him to reveal the resource for the funds that you are looking for.

I have learned that when God is in something it is easy to obtain it. I am not saying there will not ever be warfare to obtain something because I know that the enemy is an opposer. The Lord wants to bless us, but He has pre-requisites as well. 2 Corinthians 1:20 (KJB) says, "For all the promises of God in him are yea, and in him Amen, unto the glory of God by us." Worshipping the Lord for His blessings also helps us to obtain the promises. He does not want His children to suffer or lack.

CHAPTER 7

The All Sufficient One

2 Corinthians 3:5 (KJB) "Not that we are sufficient of ourselves to think anything as of ourselves: but our Sufficiency is of God."

"Sufficiency" in the Strong's Concordance is the Greek word "Hikanos." It means many, enough, worthy, long, sufficiency, and sufficient in ability. Having faith in God our Father also requires us knowing that we are not the supplier of our needs. Jehovah-Jireh is the Lord our provider. El-Shaddai is the Almighty God of Jacob, All Sufficient, and the Double Breasted One. We have a God who is able to provide for us no matter what we need and he does not need us to do anything. Learning to trust in the Lord to provide for your needs as He speaks of in Matthew 6:31(KJB), "Therefore take no thought, saying, What shall we eat? or, What shall we drink? or Wherewithal shall we be clothed?" The Scripture prior to that tells you God clothes the grass of the field, so He will also clothe you, oh ye of little faith. Reliance on Jehovah Jireh, "the Lord our provider," is pertinent to obtaining the promise or good report.

As we study the life of Jesus, the one thing He disliked the most about people was their unbelief. He would remove them from an atmosphere where He was performing miracles. If people had doubt or worry around Him, He would rebuke them and show them that He could perform the miracle because He believed in the power of God.

I believe Jesus turned the water into wine at the wedding because His mother Mary believed that he could. When she said, "Whatever he tells you to do, that do!" This was having faith in Jesus that He could do it. He did reply to his mother that it wasn't yet His time, but he still performed the miracle.

I believe that faith in God pleases Him and moves Him to perform what we ask. It is important to know who God is, how great of a Father he is and what Jesus died for, so that you will know the benefits you have access to as a believer. Knowing as much as possible about God the Father, God the Son, and God the Holy Spirit is necessary to grow in faith.

References:

Blue Letter Bible (2021). Blue Letter Bible KJV. Strong's Concordance. Retrieved from:

https://www.blueletterbible.org/lang/lexicon/lexicon.cfm?Strongs

King James Bible Online (2021). King James Bible. The Preserved and Living Word of God. Retrieved from:

https://www.kingjamesbibleonline.org

Oxford Living Dictionaries-Dissimulation definition https://en.oxforddictionaries.com/definition/dissimulation

Lexico (2021). Oxford English and Spanish Dictionary, Thesaurus, and Spanish to English Translator. Retrieved from:

https://www.lexico.com/definition/living

About The Author

NIKEYA QUICK IS A woman of
faith. She seeks to pursue the will
of God pertaining to her life. She
is taking the path that is straight and narrow,
which leads to eternal life. There is a longing for
more of God, His son Jesus and the Holy Spirit.

After going through her divorce, she decided
that Jesus Christ would be her everything. Following and trusting in Him became the new nor-
mal in her life. Her sacrifice and dedication to
God are endless.